The month of March, from the illuminated manuscript *Les Très
Riches Heures du duc de Berry*

The Story of a Special Day
Volume 83

March

23

82nd day of the year
(83rd in leap years)
283 days remaining
until the end of the year.

by Michael Dobson

Timespinner Press

Table of Contents

Cover: Patrick Henry making his "liberty or death" speech by Peter Rothermel, for the Event of the Day for March 23.

Back Cover: The month of March, from the French Gothic illuminated manuscript *Les Très Riches Heures du duc de Berry.*

March 23 Quotations

"The problem with people who have no vices is that generally you can be pretty sure they're going to have some pretty annoying virtues."

> — *actress Elizabeth Taylor, died March 23, 2011*

"The curious task of economics is to demonstrate to men how little they really know about what they imagine they can design."

> — *economist Friedrich Hayek, died March 23, 1992*

"The trouble with this country is that there are too many politicians who believe, with a conviction based on experience, that you can fool all of the people all of the time."

> — *columnist Franklin Pierce Adams (F.P.A.),*
> *died March 23, 1960*

"Human beings are unable to be honest with themselves about themselves. They cannot talk about themselves without embellishing."

> — *filmmaker Akira Kurosawa, born March 23, 1910*

"Science does not have a moral dimension. It is like a knife. If you give it to a surgeon or a murderer, each will use it differently."

> — *rocket designer Wernher von Braun, born March 23, 1912*

"Human beings are unable to be honest with themselves about themselves. They cannot talk about themselves without embellishing."

> *— filmmaker Akira Kurosawa, born March 23, 1910*

"One cannot be deeply responsive to the world without being saddened very often."

> *— psychologist Erich Fromm, born March 23, 1900*

"A wise woman never yields by appointment. It should always be an unforeseen happiness."

> *— author Stendhal, died March 23, 1842*

"I know not what course others may take; but as for me, give me liberty or give me death!"

> *— founding father Patrick Henry,*
> *speech given March 23, 1775*

"The weight of evidence for an extraordinary claim must be proportioned to its strangeness."

> *— mathematician Pierre-Simon Laplace,*
> *born March 23, 1749*

Event of the Day

"Give Me Liberty, or Give Me Death!"

Patrick Henry

Patrick Henry (May 29, 1736 — June 6, 1799) was an unsuccessful tobacco farmer and merchant who turned to the law as a career. In his first famous case, known as the "Parson's Cause," he called the king a "tyrant...who forfeits all rights to his subject's obedience" — dangerous words for the time.

He was elected to the Virginia House of Burgesses in 1765, and only nine days after being sworn in, he made an inflammatory speech condemning the Stamp Act, a British law taxing the colonists: "Caesar had his Brutus; Charles the First his Cromwell; and George the Third...may he profit by their example. *If this be treason, make the most of it!*"

Later, he had to apologize for these words, and assured the legislature that he was still loyal to the king. The final phrase became widely known and established Patrick Henry as an important leader in the colonies.

The Stamp Act was repealed, but the damage to British interests in the colonies could not be undone. Efforts began to unite the colonies around a common cause, with Patrick Henry one of Virginia's representatives.

These acts of colonial resistance resulted in Britain sending over troops to put down any attempt at rebellion. Colonial opinion at the time was divided, and Patrick Henry once again argued strongly for an aggressive response.

On March 23, 1775, Patrick Henry rose before the Virginia House of Burgesses to give a fiery speech that has forever defined his name and reputation. No contemporary account of the speech exists, and historians disagree on the accuracy of the reconstruction—among other things, some account suggest that Henry engaged in a great deal of graphic name-calling.

The last two paragraphs, and especially the final line, became famous throughout the colonies. Henry said: "If we wish to be free—if we mean to preserve inviolate those inestimable privileges for which we have been so long contending—if we mean not basely to abandon the noble struggle in which we have been so long engaged, and which we have pledged ourselves never to abandon until the glorious object of our contest shall be obtained—we must fight! ... There is no retreat but in submission and slavery! Our chains are forged! Their clanking may be heard on the plains of Boston! The war is inevitable--and let it come! I repeat it, sir, let it come. ...

"Gentlemen may cry, Peace, Peace—but there is no peace. The war is actually begun! The next gale that sweeps from the north will bring to our ears the clash of resounding arms! Our brethren are already in the field! Why stand we here idle?

What is it that gentlemen wish? What would they have? Is life so dear, or peace so sweet, as to be purchased at the price of chains and slavery? Forbid it, Almighty God! I know not what course others may take; but as for me, *give me liberty or give me death!*"

His biographer claims that the crowd jumped up and began shouting, "To Arms! To Arms!" Whether that is true or not, Virginia certainly played a critical role in the successful American Revolution. Henry served as a colonel in the war, and afterwards was the first post-colonial governor of Virginia, serving from 1776 to 1779. He also did well financially, establishing a 10,000 acre tobacco farm and acquiring 64 slaves.

Henry opposed the new U.S. Constitution, on the grounds that it gave too much power to the central government, but it passed in spite of his objections. He played a critical role in the addition of the Bill of Rights to the new constitution. He is remembered as one of the important founding fathers of the United States. Nine counties, numerous schools, ships, and military bases have been named for him. Above all, the phrase "Give me liberty or give me death" remains one of the most quoted and memorable phrases in American history.

March 23 Holidays and Celebrations

Pakistan Day (یوم پاکستان) (Pakistan)

On March 23, 1956, the British-ruled Dominion of
Pakistan became the Islamic Republic of Pakistan,
the world's first Islamic republic. Pakistan Day is
celebrated each March 23. Ceremonies include a full
military and civilian parade in the capital city of
Islamabad and the laying of wreaths at the
mausoleums of Muhammad Iqbal (محمد اقبال), who
inspired the Pakistan movement; and Muhammad Ali
Jinnah (محمد علی جناح), known as *Baba-i-Qaum*, or
Father of the Nation.

Pakistani schoolgirls at the Tomb of Quaid.
Photo: Kashif Mardani

Day of Hungarian-Polish Friendship (Hungary and Poland)

A Polish proverb and a Hungarian proverb both speak to the special relationship between the two nations. Poles say, *Polak, Węgier — dwa bratanki, i do szabli, i do szklanki,oba zuchy, oba żwawi, niech im Pan Bóg błogosławi.* ("Pole and Hungarian cousins be, good for fight and good for party Both are valiant, both are lively; upon them may God's blessings be.") In Hungary, the expression is *Lengyel, magyar — két jó barát, együtt harcol s issza borát.* ("Pole and Hungarian — two good friends. Together they battle and drink their wine.")

Dia del Mar (Bolivia)

In Bolivia, March 23 is known as *Dia del Mar*, or the "Day of the Sea." It commemorates the loss of the "Litoral," a region of 120,000 square kilometers that Bolivia lost to Chile in the 1879. The specific date of March 23 refers to the Bolivian defeat at the Battle of Calama (also known as the Battle of Topáter), in which a small group of Bolivian soldiers commanded by Eduardo Abaroa faced a much larger Chilean force. The Chileans demanded that Abaroa surrender, but Abaroa replied, "Me surrender? Tell your grandmother to surrender!" after which he was shot dead. On the Day of the Sea, flowers are laid at the statue of Eduardo Abaroa in La Paz; there are military parades, dances, and street fairs throughout the country; and a national beauty pageant names Miss Litoral.

Dia del Mar parade. Photo: Pedro Szekely

Otago Anniversary Day (New Zealand)

Otago Anniversary Day celebrates two events: the arrival of the first ship of Scottish settlers (including the founder of the Otago settlement, Captain William Cargill) in New Zealand on March 23, 1848, and the establishment of the Otago provincial government on March 23, 1852.

World Meteorological Day (International)

The World Meteorological Organization (WMO) is the United Nations organization for weather and climate, with 191 nations taking part. It sponsors World Meteorological Day on March 23.

Lieldienas (ancient Latvia)

In ancient Latvia, a three or four day celebration of
the vernal equinox began on March 23. Lieldienas
observances included scaring birds away from homes.
and giving eggs, with the proverb:: "One who steals
an egg will be poor. One who eats a hard-boiled egg
without salt is a liar. A girl who gives a boy two eggs
doesn't like him; three eggs mean there is a chance
she likes; four eggs means she doesn't like him but
will be with him because he is richer; five eggs means
she loves him."

Tubilustrium (ancient Rome)

In ancient Rome, Tubilustrium was the last day of
the festival of Quinquatria, sacred to Minerva,
goddess of wisdom. On Tubilustrium, the trumpets
used in sacred rites were ritually purified.

Easter Season

Easter is a "moveable feast," meaning it occurs on
different days each year. The earliest date for Easter
is March 22. See the Easter Events section for more
details.

Christian Feast Days

March 22 is the feast day of Rafqa Pietra Choboq
Ar-Rayés and Turibius de Mongrovejo. In Eastern
Christianity, it's the commemoration of Saint Nicon
of the Kiev Caves and Saint Basil of Mangazea. and
of martyrs Philetas the Senator, Dometius of
Phrygia, and Luke the New of Mytilcne.

What Happened on March 23?

The abbreviation "O.S." on some dates refers to the fact that the Russian Empire did not switch from the Julian to the Gregorian calendar at the same time as the rest of Europe, and therefore some figures have two dates for their birth or death.

People whose original names are not in the Western alphabet have their native names in the appropriate script shown in parenthesis.

1400 CE – **End of the Trần Dynasty**

The Trần Dynasty, which ruled Vietnam from 1225 CE to 1400, was considered a golden age of music and culture for its dance and theater, and was noted for reforms in politics and taxation. Technological innovations included the introduction of gunpowder and paper money, along with developments in medicine. The dynasty repelled three invasions by the Mongols.

The Trần dynasty ended on March 23, 1400 CE, when Hồ Quý Ly overthrew the five-year old emperor, Trần Thiếu Đế, and established the Hồ Dynasty with himself as the new emperor.

1708 CE – The "Old Pretender" Returns

The Wars of Religion in England between Protestants and Catholics extended to the royal succession. King James II was deposed as last Catholic king of England, and the throne went to William of Orange and his wife Mary.

James II had a son, James Francis Edward Stuart (the "Old Pretender, left") who declared himself rightful king of England on the death of his father. James was recognized by France and Spain, and tried to invade England with a French fleet on March 23, 1708. The British Navy stopped him, and he spent the rest of his life in exile.

His son, known as Bonnie Prince Charlie (the "Young Pretender") would also try to take the throne in 1745. Neither were successful, and the Hanoverian line would rule England through the reign of Queen Victoria, who died in 1901.

1801 CE – **Assassination of Tsar Paul I**

Paul I (Па́вел I Петро́вич), Tsar of Russia following his mother Catherine the Great, attempted major changes in Russia. He reversed some of the harsher policies of his mother, tried to reform the Russian nobility with a code of chivalry, introduced Prussian military discipline, fought corruption in the Russian treasury, and reversed some of his mother's expansionist foreign policies. He was also personally eccentric, and some thought he was mad.

Opposition to his rule built, and finally, a band of officers whom Paul I had dismissed from the military attacked the Tsar in his bedroom on the night of March 23 [O.S. March 11], 1801. They tried to force him to sign an abdication decree, and when he refused, they stabbed him with a sword, strangled him, and trampled him to death.

1806 CE – **The Lewis and Clark Expedition Heads Back**

Two years after the Meriwether Lewis and William Clark Expedition began its long trek across the North American continent, they decided to start their return journey on March 23, 1806.

The expedition members all voted on whether it was time to turn back, including the Shoshone woman Sacagawea and Clark's slave York, making the occasion the first time in American history in which a woman and a slave were permitted to have an equal vote.

1857 CE – **First Otis Elevator**

Inventor Elisha Otis invented the "safety elevator," which prevents an elevator from falling even if its hoisting cable should fail. He first demonstrated his invention at the 1854 New York World's Fair by having the only rope holding up his elevator platform cut with an axe. The very first Otis safety elevator was installed at 488 Broadway, New York City, on March 23, 1857.

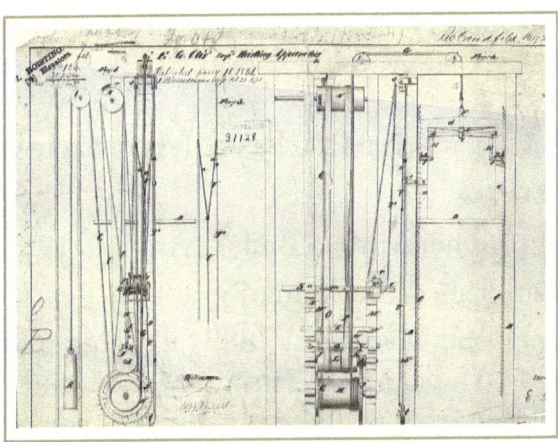

Otis Elevator patent drawing, showing the first safety catch to protect against a broken cable

1862 CE – **First Battle of Kernstown**

On March 23, 1862, Stonewall Jackson attacked what he thought was a small Union detachment that turned out to be a full infantry division. He was driven from the field, but his tactical defeat turned into strategic victory, because it prevented the Union from transferring forces to the Peninsula Campaign against Richmond.

1868 CE – **Founding of the University of California**

On March 23, 1868, the Organic Act created the University of California, built on an existing private institution, the College of California. It now consists of ten campuses with over 200, 000 students, and is regarded as one of the top public university systems in the world.

1889 CE – **Ahmadiyya Movement Founded**

Indian prophet Mirza Ghulam Ahmad (ميرزا غلام أحمد) established the Ahmadiyya (أحمدية) movement on March 23, 1889, claiming to be the Christian Messiah, the Muslim Mahdi, and the Hindu Avatar of Kalki. Ahmadiyya is considered heretical by many Muslims, and in Pakistan it is a crime for an Ahmadi to self-identify as Muslim.

1905 CE – **Theriso Revolt (Η Επανάσταση του Θερίσου) Begins**

The island nation of Crete had been under Ottoman rule for more than a century, but the island's Christian majority wanted to become part of Greece. On March 23 [O.S. March 10], 1905, Cretan politician Eleftherios Venizelos (λευθέριος Βενιζέλος) led a rebellion of some 1,500 Cretans to overthrow the Ottoman-appointed government. A semi-civil war broke out, resulting in a brokered peace when the government adopted many of the proposed Theriso reforms and offered amnesty to the rebels. Finally, in 1913, Crete became part of Greece, and Venizelos became Greece's prime minister.

1909 CE – **Teddy Roosevelt Goes on Safari**

Shortly after the end of his presidency, Theodore Roosevelt went on a safari in east and central Africa, sponsored by the Smithsonian Institution and the American Museum of Natural History. Leaving on March 23, 1909, and returning over a year later, Roosevelt and his party killed or trapped over 11,000 animals, ranging from insects to elephants.

Teddy Roosevelt with dead elephant

1933 CE – **Hitler Becomes Dictator**

On March 23, 1933, the German Reichstag
passed and the German President signed a bill
named *Gesetz zur Behebung der Not von Volk und Reich*
("Law to Remedy the Distress of the People and
the Nation"), commonly known as the Enabling
Act of 1933, which allowed Hitler's cabinet to
enact laws without the participation of the
Reichstag. Although technically ultimate power
did not rest with Hitler alone, the cabinet met
only occasionally and in practice a decree of
Adolf Hitler was automatically a German law.

1939 CE – **The Little War**

In the period leading up to the start of World War II in Europe, a brief war took place between the First Slovak Republic and Hungary. At dawn on March 23, 1939, Hungarian troops rolled over the Slovak border. Although the Slovak Republic was nominally under the protection of Germany, the Germans hampered their forces even further, and the Slovaks sued for peace, ceding a strip of eastern Slovak territory to Hungary.

1965 CE – **Gemini 3 Lifts Off**

Gemini 3 (right), the first manned mission in the Gemini program and the seventh manned U.S. spaceflight, was notable as the first manned spacecraft to perform an orbital maneuver, changing the shape of their orbit and dropping to a lower altitude. Astronauts Gus Grissom and John Young flew the mission.

Grissom, whose Mercury spacecraft Liberty Bell 7 sank after splashdown, named the Gemini 3 craft "Molly Brown," in reference to the musical "The Unsinkable Molly Brown." When NASA management objected, Grissom proposed naming it "Titanic" instead. It was, however, the last Gemini flight the astronauts were allowed to name themselves.

1982 CE – **Coup in Guatemala**

On March 23, 1982, a coup d'état led by General Efraín Ríos Montt overthrew the president, suspended the constitution, and started a campaign against dissidents. Although supported by the Reagan Administration, Ríos Montt was forced from office in 1983, but remained a political power even after being charged with crimes against humanity. He was placed under house arrest in 2012 and scheduled for trial.

1989 CE – **Cold Fusion Announced**

On March 23, 1989, scientists Stanley Pons and Martin Fleischmann announced the development of "cold fusion," a type of nuclear reaction that could take place at room temperature as opposed to the extreme temperatures required for convention "hot" fusion.

Although their announcement drew widespread interest because of the great potential of such a development, scientists were unable to duplicate the experiment and the claims are generally considered to have been debunked. A small amount of research into low-energy nuclear reactions (LENR) continues, but without notable success.

1991 CE – **Sierra Leone Civil War Begins**

On March 23, 1991, revolutionary troops supported by the Liberian special forces invaded the Sierra Leone to overthrow its government, triggering a civil war that lasted 11 years, devastated the country, and killed over 50,000.

1994 CE – **Green Ramp Disaster**

A mid-air collision between an F-16 and a C-130 over Pope Air Force base turned into the worst peacetime loss of life suffered by the 82nd Airborne Division when the F-16 plowed into the aircraft parking area known as the Green Ramp, puncturing the fuel tanks in a C-141. The resultant fireball killed 24 and injured 80. All casualties were on the ground; the F-16 crew ejected and the C-130 was not hurt badly enough to crash.

2001 CE – **End of the *Mir* Space Station**

Nearing the end of its useful life, the Soviet space station *Mir* (Мир) was successfully deorbited and crashed into the Pacific Ocean over a period of several days, ending on March 23, 2001. It had been operating since February 20, 1986, establishing a record for the longest human presence in space, of 3,644 days and a record for the longest single human spaceflight of 437 days, held by Valeri Polyakov.

Mir Space Station seen from the Space Shuttle *Discovery*

Who Was Born on March 23?

Arts, Fashion, and Literature

Kenneth Cole (March 23, 1954 —)

Clothing designer Kenneth Cole founded the American fashion house that bears his name.

Kim Stanley Robinson (March 23, 1952 —)

Science fiction writer Kim Stanley Robins is best known for his *Mars* trilogy, which received two Hugo Awards and a Nebula Award.

H. Beam Piper (March 23, 1904 — circa November 6, 1964)

Science fiction writer and railroad worker H. Beam Piper is famed for such works as *Lord Kalvan of Otherwhen* and *Little Fuzzy*. He committed suicide in November 1964, but his body was not found immediately, making the exact date of his death uncertain.

Erich Fromm (March 23, 1900 — March 18, 1980)

Psychologist and philosopher Erich Fromm is known for his international bestseller *The Art of Loving* and for his 1941 work *Escape From Freedom*.

Juan Gris (March 23, 1887 — May 11, 1927)

Spanish painter and sculptor Juan Gris played a major role in the emergence of Cubism.

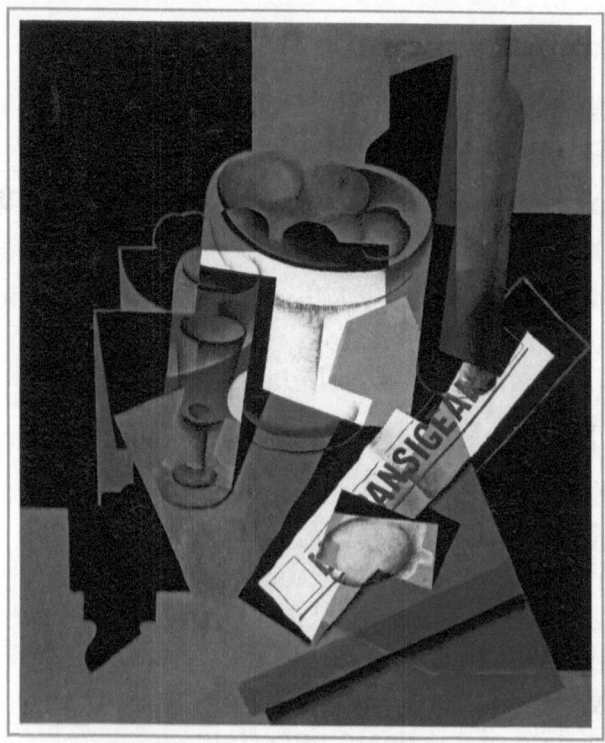

Still Life With Newspaper, Juan Gris

Josef Čapek (March 23, 1887 — April 1945)

Czech writer, poet, and cartoonist Josef Čapek invented the word "robot," used by his brother Karel Čapek in his famous play *R.U.R.*. ("Robot" comes from the Czech "robota," meaning forced labor.) He was arrested after the German invasion of Czechoslovakia and died in Bergen-Belsen concentration camp.

J. C. Leyendecker (March 23, 1874 — July 25, 1951)

American illustrator J. C. Leyendecker created the Arrow Collar Man and produced over 300 covers for *The Saturday Evening Post*. He is credited as having "virtually invented the whole idea of modern magazine design," and as a major influence on Norman Rockwell.

Business and Industry

Bette Nesmith Graham (March 23, 1924 — May 12, 1980)

Typist and commercial artist Bette Nesmith Graham invented Liquid Paper typewriter correction fluid. She was also the mother of Michael Nesmith, best known as a member of The Monkees.

"Weapons for Liberty," by J. C. Leyendecker

G. D. Naidu (**March 23, 1893 — January 4, 1974**)

Indian inventor and engineer Naidu manufactured the first electric motor in India, and made contributions in agriculture, automobiles, and film.

Calouste Gulbenkian (**March 23, 1869 — July 20, 1955**)

Armenia businessman Gulbenkian helped arrange the merger of Royal Dutch Petroleum and Shell Transport, creating Royal Dutch Shell, and also built the Turkish and Iraqi Petroleum Company. He left an extensive art collection and established a foundation with a large part of his fortune, estimated at up to US$840 million.

Film and Television

Nicholle and David Tom (**March 23, 1978 —)**

The Tom twins are both actors, along with another sister, Heather Tom. Nicholle was featured in 1992's *Beethoven* and its sequel, and on the sitcom *The Nanny*. David Tom is best known as Billy Abbott on *The Young and the Restless*, where his sister Heather also played the role of Victoria.

Keri Russell (March 23, 1976 —)

Russell won a Golden Globe for playing the title role on TV's *Felicity* and has appeared in numerous films.

Keri Russell (Photo: Joella Marano)

Michelle Monaghan (March 23, 1976 —)

Actress Monaghan had a starring role in the TV series *Boston Public*, and has been featured in *The Heartbreak Kid, Mission: Impossible III*, and many other roles.

Judith Godréche (March 23, 1972 —)

French actress Godréche is best known to American audiences for co-starring with Leonardo DiCaprio and Jeremy Irons in 1998's *The Man in the Iron Mask.*

Marin Hinkle (March 23, 1966 —)

Hinkle had feature roles on the sitcom *Two and a Half* Men, and on the TV dramas *Once and Again* and *Deception.*

Richard Grieco (March 23, 1965 —)

Former model Grieco played Rick Gardner on *One Life to Live*, Detective Booker on *21 Jump Street* and its spinoff *Booker,* and played himself in 1998's *A Night at the Roxbury.*

Sarah G. Buxton (March 23, 1965 —)

Buxton was an original cast member of the soap opera *Sunset Beach*, and also appeared on the soaps *The Bold and the Beautiful* and *Days of Our Lives.*

Hope Davis (March 23, 1964 —)

Davis received a Golden Globe nomination for her role in *American Splendor* and an Emmy nomination for playing Hillary Rodham Clinton in *The Special Relationship.*

Catherine Keener (March 23, 1959 —)

Keener received Academy Award nominations for her roles in *Being John Malkovich* and *Capote*.

Amanda Plummer (March 23, 1957 —)

Plummer is known for such films as 1994's *Pulp Fiction* and 1991's *The Fisher King*.

Teresa Ganzel (March 23, 1957 —)

Comedienne Ganzel is best known for playing ditzy, busty blonde bimbo roles in such films as *The Toy* and *National Lampoon's Movie Madness*. She replaced Carol Wayne as the Matinee Lady in the *Tonight Show Starring Johnny Carson* "Tea Time Movie" skits, and appeared on game shows including *The $25,000* (and *$100,000) Pyramid* and *Hollywood Squares*.

Corinne Cléry (March 23, 1950 —)

Cléry starred in 1975's *Story of O*, and was a Bond girl in 1979's *Moonraker*.

Barbara Rhoades (March 23, 1947 —)

Rhoades acted in *The Shakiest Gun in the West, Up the Sandbox, The Choirboys*, and *Harry and Tonto*. She also had featured roles in the TV series *Soap* and *One Life to Live*.

Michael Haneke (March 23, 1942 —)

Austrian filmmaker Haneke's 2012 film *Amour* received five Academy Award Nominations and also won the Palme d'Or at the Cannes Film Festival.

Mark Rydell (March 23, 1934 —)

Rydell played Walt Johnson on *The Edge of Night* and Jeff Baker on *As the World Turns*, and acted in films by Roger Altman and Woody Allen. He received an Oscar nomination for directing *On Golden Pond*.

David Watkin (March 23, 1925 — February 19, 2008)

Cinematographer Watkin won an Academy Award for *Out of Africa*, and is famous for staging and filming the beach running scene in *Chariots of Fire*.

Ugo Tognazzi (March 23, 1922 — October 27, 1990)

Italian actor Tognazzi is known for his work in numerous Italian comedy films, winning the Best Male Actor Award at the Cannes Film Festival for his work in Bernado Bertolucci's *La tragedia di un uomo ridiolo*. He is best known to American audiences for his roles in *Barbarella* and the French comedy *La Cage aux Folles*.

Marty Allen (March 23, 1922 —)

Comedian and actor Marty Allen recorded a number of comedy albums, appeared on the *Ed Sullivan Show* 40 times, and made hundreds of television appearances, including numerous game shows.

Marty Allen

Akira Kurosawa (黒澤 明) (March 23, 1910 — September 6, 1998)

Widely considered one of the most important filmmakers in the history of the cinema, Japanese director Akira Kurosawa is known for such classics as *Seven Samurai, Yojimbo, Kagemusha,* and *Ran.*

Joan Crawford (March 23, either 1905 or 1908 — May 10, 1977)

Voted among the top ten greatest female American film stars by the American Film Institute, Joan Crawford was one of the top movie stars of the 1930s. She won an Academy Award for 1945's *Mildred Pierce,* and is also known as the subject of the book and movie *Mommie Dearest,* alleging she abused her adopted daughter.

Joan Crawford in *The Last of Mrs. Cheyney* (1937)

Dora Gerson (March 23, 1899 — February 14, 1943)

Jewish German cabaret singer and silent film actress Dora Gerson was murdered along with her family at Auschwitz.

Cedric Gibbons (March 23, 1893 — July 26, 1960)

Art director and production designer Cedric Gibbons not only designed the Oscar statuette, but also won 11 Academy Awards for art direction out of 39 total nominations. His Oscar-winning films include such classics as 1940's *Pride and Prejudice*, 1944's *Gaslight*, and 1951's *An American in Paris*.

Music

Chaka Khan (March 23, 1953 —)

Chaka Khan won ten Grammy Awards for her solo work and for her work with the funk band Rufus. Her hits include "Tell Me Something Good, "Sweet Thing," and "I Feel for You."

Ric Ocasek (March 23, 1949 —)

Ocasek is best known as lead vocalist and guitarist for The Cars.

David Grisman (March 23, 1945 —)

Mandolin player David Grisman mixed bluegrass and Hot Club of Paris-influenced jazz into a unique style called "Dawg Music. He was a close friend of Grateful Dead musician Jerry Garcia and played on the Dead album *American Beauty*.

Lale Andersen (March 23, 1905 — August 29, 1972)

German chanson singer Lale Andersen is best remembered for her cover of "Lili Marleen," which became a popular song on both sides during World War II in Europe.

Ludwig Minkus (Людвиг Минкус) (March 23, 1826 — December 7, 1917)

Austrian composer Minkus is known for his ballet compositions, including the *Grand Pas classique*, *Pas de trois* and *Mazurka des enfants,* which remain part of the traditional classical ballet repertory.

Newsmakers

Princess Eugenie of York (March 23, 1990 —)

Princess Eugenie of York is the younger daughter of Prince Andrew and Sarah, Duchess of York, and sixth in line to the throne of England.

Perez Hilton (March 23, 1978 —)

Blogger and television personality Mario Lavandeira, Jr., better known as "Perez Hilton" (a pun on "Paris Hilton"), is known for celebrity gossip.

Jayson Blair (March 23, 1976 —)

Former journalist Jayson Blair is known for resigning from *The New York Times* after charges of plagiarism and fabrication in his stories.

Karen McDougal (March 23, 1971 —)

McDougal was *Playboy* Magazine's Playmate of the Year for 1998.

Vasily Zaytsev (Василий Зайцев) (March 23, 1915 — December 15, 1991)

Soviet military sniper Zaytsev was famous for the Battle of Stalingrad, in which he killed 225 Axis soldiers. He is portrayed in the book and movie *Enemy at the Gates*.

Milbourne Christopher (March 23, 1914 — June 17, 1984)

Illusionist and magic historian Milbourne Christopher was president of the Society of American Magicians and a founder of the Committee for Skeptical Inquiry. He is the namesake of the Milbourne Christopher Awards awarded to performing magicians and illusionists.

Joseph Boxhall (March 23, 1884 — April 25, 1967)

Boxhall was the Fourth Officer aboard RMS *Titanic*. He calculated the *Titanic's* position so distress signals could be sent, tried to signal a passing ship to no avail, and as officer aboard Lifeboat No. 2, spotted RMS *Carpathia* and guided her to the lifeboats with a flare.

Nathaniel Reed (March 23, 1862 — January 7, 1950)

"Texas Jack" Reed led a bandit gang in stagecoach, bank, and train robberies, rode with the Dalton gang, and helped Cherokee Bill escape from Fort Smith. After serving a year in prison, he became an evangelist preaching against a life of crime and toured with Wild West shows. He published a memoir, *The Life of Texas Jack*, which is highly collectable today.

Politics

Ludwig Quidde (March 23, 1858 — March 4, 1941)

German pacifist Ludwig Quidde won the 1927 Nobel Peace Prize. In the Bismarck era; he went to jail for criticizing Kaiser Wilhelm II;

supported efforts to avoid World War II during
the Weimar Republic; and finally escaped to
Switzerland following Adolf Hitler's rise to
power.

Schuyler Colfax (March 23, 1823 — January 13, 1885)

Colfax (right), vice-president of the United States under Ulysses S. Grant, is one of only two Americans to have been both Speaker of the House and Vice President. Grant and Colfax were the youngest President/Vice President team until the inauguration of Bill Clinton and Al Gore in 1993.

Science and Technology

Robert Gallo (March 23, 1937 —)

Gallo played an important role in discovering HIV, the infectious agent responsible for AIDS. His story is part of the book and TV drama *And the Band Played On.*

Ludvig Faddeev (Людвиг Фаддёев) (March 23, 1934 —)

Theoretical physicist and mathematician Faddeev is known for discovering the Faddeev equations in quantum mechanics, for the Faddeev-Popov ghosts, and for his work in the development of the quantum inverse scattering method.

Philip Zimbardo (March 23, 1933 —)

Psychologist Zimbardo is best known for the Stanford prison study in 1971, and for his books *The Lucifer Effect* and *The Time Paradox.*

Wernher von Braun (March 23, 1912 — June 16, 1977)

A leader in the development of rocket technology, Wernher von Braun developed the V-1 and V-2 rockets for Nazi Germany, and subsequently served as chief of NASA's Marshall Space Flight Center, where he developed the Saturn V launch vehicle.

Wernher von Braun

Daniel Bovet (March 23, 1907 — April 8, 1992)

Nobel-prize winning pharmacologist Daniel Bovet discovered antihistamines.

Emmy Noether (March 23, 1882 — April 14, 1935)

German mathematician Emmy Noether revolutionized the theories of rings, fields, and algebras, and established Noether's theorem, which explains the fundamental connection between symmetry and conservation laws. She left Germany after Hitler's rise to power and spent the rest of her life in the United States.

Hermann Staudinger (March 23, 1881 — September 8, 1965)

Staudinger won the 1953 Nobel Prize in Chemistry for demonstrating the existence of macromolecules, or polymers, and establishing the field of polymer chemistry.

William Smith (March 23, 1769 — August 28, 1939)

Smith, known as the "father of English geology" for creating the first nationwide geological map of England and Wales, was initially overlooked by the scientific community because of his humble origins. His work was plagiarized and he was financially ruined, spending time in debtor's prison, before earning recognition late in life.

Pierre-Simon Laplace (March 23, 1749 — March 5, 1827)

Laplace, considered one of the greatest scientist in history, brought calculus to celestial mechanics, formulated Laplace's equation and the Laplace transform, postulated black holes and gravitational collapse, and developed what is now known as the Bayesian approach to probability. He was appointed French minister of the interior by Napoléon and subsequently appointed a senator

Sports

Kyrie Irving (March 23, 1992 —)

Kyrie Irving won the NBA Rookie of the Year Award in 2012.

Mo Farah (March 23, 1983 —)

Track and field athlete Mo Farah won two Olympic gold medals, and was named 2011 European Athlete of the Year.

Dougie Lampkin (March 23, 1976 —)

Motorcycle trials rider Lampkin won sixteen world championships, six British championships, and two Spanish championships.

Chris Hoy (March 23, 1976 —)

Track bicyclist Chris Hoy won six gold Olympic medals, becoming the most successful Olympic cyclist of all time.

Jason Kidd (March 23, 1973 —)

Basketball player Kidd has played for the Dallas Mavericks, Phoenix Suns, New Jersey Nets, and New York Knicks, winning numerous honors.

Joe Calzaghe (March 23, 1972 —)

Boxer Calzaghe was Super Middleweight Champion of the WBO, IBA, WBA, WBC, and *The Ring*.

Joe Calzaghe (Photo: Ben Duffy, Ian Monk Associates)

Steve Redgrave (March 23, 1962 —)

British rower Steve Redgrave won a record five gold medals in consecutive Olympic Games from 1984 to 2000.

Moses Malone (March 23, 1955 —)

Basketball Hall of Famer Moses Malone was named one of the 50 greatest players in the NBA.

Geno Auriemma (March 23, 1954 —)

College basketball coach Geno Auriemma led the University of Connecticut to seven NCAA Division I national championships, and led the U.S. women's national basketball team to a gold medal at the 2012 Summer Olympics. He was inducted into the Basketball Hall of Fame in 2006.

Bo Díaz (March 23, 1953 — November 23, 1990)

MLB catcher Bo Díaz was inducted into the Venezuelan Baseball Hall of Fame and Museum in 2006.

Ron Jaworski (March 23, 1951 —)

Former quarterback Ron Jaworski, known as "Jaws" and the "Polish Rifle," became an NFL analyst for ESPN.

Craig Breedlove (March 23, 1937 —)

Breedlove set five world land speed records, breaking the 400 mph, 500 mph, and 600 mph marks in a variety of turbojet powered vehicles, all named *Spirit of America*. The Beach Boys' song "Spirit of America" is about him.

Yevgeny Grishin (Евгений Гришин) (March 23, 1931 — July 9, 2005)

Russian speed skater Yevgeny Grishin set seven world records during his career, and won four gold Olympic medals in the 1956 and 1960 Winter Olympics.

Roger Bannister (March 23, 1929 —)

English runner Roger Bannister is known for becoming the first person to run a mile in less than four minutes.

Donald Campbell (March 23, 1921 — January 4, 1967)

Racing driver Donald Campbell broke eight world speed records in the 1950s and 1960s, and is the only person to have set both world land and water speed records in the same year.

Who Died on March 23?

Arts, Fashion, and Literature

Christóbal Balenciaga (January 21, 1895 — March 23, 1972)

Fashion designer Balenciaga founded the fashion house bearing his name.

Edwin O'Connor (July 29, 1918 — March 23, 1968)

O'Connor won the 1962 Pulitzer Prize for Fiction for his novel *The Edge of Sadness*.

Franklin Pierce Adams (November 15, 1881 — March 23, 1960)

Known by his initials, F.P.A. was a newspaper columnist of the 1920s and 1930s and a member of the informal Algonquin Round Table. His newspaper column featured work by Robert Benchley, Dorothy Parker, and James Thurber.

Paul César Helleu (December 17, 1859 — March 23, 1927)

Helleu was best known for his Belle Époque portraits of society women, and for the ceiling mural of the night sky constellations in New York City's Grand Central Terminal.

La Duchesse de Marlborough, Consuelo Vanderbilt
by Paul César Helleu

Stendhal (January 23, 1783 — March 23, 1842)

Marie-Henri Beyle, better known by his pseudonym Stendhal, was an 19th century French writer considered one of the foremost early practitioners of realism. His most famous book is 1839's *The Charterhouse of Parma*.

Film and Theater

Elizabeth Taylor (February 27, 1932 — March 23, 2011)

Considered one of the greatest screen actresses of the Golden Age of Hollywood, Taylor won Oscars for her roles in *BUtterfield 8* and *Who's Afraid of Virginia Woolf?* She was famously married eight times to seven husbands.

Giuletta Masina (February 22, 1921 — March 23, 1994)

Masina starred in two Academy Award-winning foreign films, *La Strada* and *Nights of Cabiria*, and won Best Actress at the 1957 Cannes Film Festival for the latter.

Elizabeth Taylor

Del Lord (October 7, 1894 — March 23, 1970)

Lord is best known for directing more than three dozen *Three Stooges* films, and also played the driver of the police van in the *Keystone Cops* films.

Mae Murray (May 10, 1889 — March 23, 1965)

Silent film star Mae Murray was known as "the girl with the bee-stung lips." Her best known role was in 1925's *The Merry Widow*, directed by Erich von Stroheim.

Mae Murray in *Broadway Rose* (1922)

Peter Lorre (June 26, 1904 — March 23, 1964)

Peter Lorre's breakthrough role was as a serial killer in the 1931 German film *M*. He later appeared in such classics as *Casablanca* and *The Maltese Falcon*.

Caricature of Peter Lorre from Tex Avery's *Hollywood Steps Out*

Music

Cindy Walker (July 20, 1918 — March 23, 2006)

Singer-songwriter Cindy Walker was inducted into the Country Music Fall of Fame in 1997.

Her hits (for herself and others) include "You Don't Know Me," Dream Baby (How Long Must I Dream)," and "In the Misty Moonlight."

Eileen Farrell (February 13, 1920 — March 23, 2002)

America soprano Eileen Farrell performed both classical and popular music, known for her 1940s weekly radio program *Eileen Farrell Sings*. She performed five seasons with the Metropolitan Opera, and crossed over to popular music with 1960's *I've Got a Right to Sing the Blues*.

Politics, Journalism, Economics

Desmond Doss (February 7, 1919 — March 23, 2006)

Combat medic Doss was the first conscientious objector to receive the Medal of Honor, and the subject of an award-winning documentary.

David McTaggart (June 24, 1932 — March 23, 2001)

Former badminton champion McTaggart was chairman and chief spokesman for Greenpeace.

Rowland Evans (April 28, 1921 — March 23, 2001)

Evans was best known for his long-running newspaper column with Robert Novak, and for his regular appearances on TV news programs.

Luis Donaldo Colosio (February 10, 1950 — March 23, 1994)

Mexican presidential candidate Colosio was assassinated at a campaign rally in Tijuana.

Friedrich Hayek (May 8, 1899 — March 23, 1992)

Hayek shared the 1974 Nobel Prize in Economics and is known for his book *The Road to Serfdom*.

Arthur M. Okun (November 28, 1928 — March 23, 1980)

Economist Okun developed Okun's Law: for every 1% increase in unemployment, a country's GDP will be 2% lower than its potential.

Bhagat Singh (September 28, 1907 — March 23, 1931)
Shivaram Hari Rajguru (August 24, 1908 — March 23, 1931)
Sukhdev Thapar (May 15, 1907 — March 23, 1931)

Indian revolutionaries Singh, Rajguru, and Thapar were executed for the assassination of

Deputy Police Superintendent J. P. Saunders in response to the death of movement leader Lala Lajpat Rai while in police custody.

Charles Carroll (March 22, 1723 — March 23, 1783)

Maryland politician Carroll was a delegate to the Continental Congress and built the mansion Mount Clare, which is now a museum.

Religion

Said Nursî (1878 — March 23, 1960)

Turkish Sunni Islamic theologian Bediüzzaman Said Nursî wrote the 6,000 page *Risale-I Nur* collection of Qur'anic commentary. The faith movement based on his work has millions of members worldwide.

Saint Rafka (June 29, 1832 — March 23, 1914)

Lebanese Maronite nun Rafqa Pietra Choboq Ar-Rayès (رفقا بطرسيّة شبق ألريّس) was canonized by Pope John Paul II in 2001.

March: The Third Month

"Up from the sea, the wild north wind is blowing
Under the sky's gray arch;
Smiling I watch the shaken elm boughs, knowing
It is the wind of March."

— *"March," John Greenleaf Whittier*

In ancient Rome, March was the first month of the year. As the first month of spring, in the Mediterranean climate it marked the beginning of the military campaign season. That's why March (Martius) is named in honor of Mars, the Roman god of war.

Although the first month of the year was moved back to January sometime during the transition of Rome from a kingdom to a republic (historians differ), March was the first month of the year in Russia until the end of the 15th Century, and is the first month of the year in many other cultures and religions.

In the northern hemisphere, March 1 marks the beginning of meteorological spring. In the southern hemisphere, March is the equivalent of September, making southern hemisphere March the beginning of autumn.

March is one of the seven months that have 31 days in it. March starts on the same day of the week as November every year, and except for leap years starts on the same day as February. March starts on the same day of the week as the previous June except for leap years, and in leap years starts on the same day as the previous September and December.

March in Other Cultures

In Finland, March is called *maaliskuu* (earthy month). In Ukraine, it's *березень* (birch tree). Other names for March include *Lentmonat* (Saxon), *Hyld-monath* (Angles), and *sušec* (Slovene).

March Symbols

Birthstones: Aquamarine (right) and bloodstone, both representing courage.

Birth Flowers: Daffodils

March Events

Honorary months

Presidents, Congresses, and nations around the world issue proclamations recognizing particular months to honor certain causes. These events generally fall in March. (All US unless otherwise noted.)

National Nutrition Month

American Red Cross Month

Women's History Month (celebrated in Canada during October)

Irish-American Heritage Month

Colorectal Cancer Awareness Month

Fire Prevention Month (The Philippines)

"March Madness" (United States)

The NCAA Men's Division I Basketball Championship, popularly known as "March Madness" or the "Big Dance," is a single-elimination tournament to establish the champion college basketball team.

Earth Hour (International)

On Earth Hour, held on the last Saturday of March each year, households and business are urged to turn off all non-essential lights for one hour between 8:30pm to 9:30pm on each person's local time. The goal is to raise awareness of the need to take action on climate change.

Easter Events

La crucifixión by El Greco

Easter Season

The Christian holiday of Easter in Western
Christianity is held on the first Sunday after the
Paschal Full Moon following the March equinox,
which is officially set at March 21 by church
reckoning. Easter itself can therefore occur as
early as March 22 and as late as April 25, but
occurs most often in April. In Eastern
Christianity, which uses the Julian calendar,
Easter occurs between April 4 and May 8. This
also sets the date for the various events that lead
up to Easter, most importantly the events of Holy
Week.

Passion Sunday

The fifth Sunday of the Christian season of Lent
is known as Passion Sunday in various Protestant
denominations and by some traditionalist
Catholics. Sometimes, the sixth Sunday of Lent
is referred to as Passion Sunday, but it is more
commonly known as Palm Sunday. Passion
Sunday starts the two-week Passiontide, which
ends on Holy Saturday, the day before Easter,
commemorating the day that Jesus's body was
laid in the tomb. The fifth Sunday of Lent can
occur as early as March 8 (though the next time
it will be that early is in 2285 CE), and as late as
April 11.

Palm Sunday

The moveable feast of Palm Sunday commemorates the triumphant entry of Jesus into Jerusalem, an event mentioned in all four gospels. In many Christian churches, palm leaves are distributed to the worshippers. The earliest date for Palm Sunday is March 15, and the latest is April 18.

Maundy Thursday

The Thursday before Easter is Maundy Thursday, when the Last Supper took place. Because of its relation to Easter, the earliest day it can occur is March 19, and the latest it can occur is April 22.

Good Friday

Good Friday, observed during Holy Week on the Friday preceding Easter Sunday, commemorates the crucifixion of Jesus and his death at Calvary. Because of its relation to Easter, the earliest day it can occur is March 20, and the latest it can occur is April 23.

Holy Saturday

Sometimes called Easter Eve or Black Saturday, Holy Saturday commemorates the day in which Jesus's body lay in the tomb.

Some mistakenly refer to this day as "Easter Saturday," but that properly describes the Saturday following Easter, the last day of Easter Week. The earliest it can occur is March 21, and the latest it can occur is April 24.

Easter

Easter celebrates the resurrection of Jesus Christ on the third day after his crucifixion. In the liturgical calendar, Easter follows the season of Lent, and begins the period known as Eastertide, which ends on Pentecost Sunday.

Easter is observed religiously in a morning service. In the U.S., it's also common to decorate Easter eggs (right) and make Easter  baskets of eggs and candy, often with the Easter bunny as a symbol. The White House traditionally hosts an egg hunt, and many communities have Easter parades.

Easter customs around the world include bonfires (Cyprus, western Sweden), egg fighting (Bulgaria), cross-country skiing and reading murder mysteries (Norway), and children dressed as witches collecting candy door-to-door (other Nordic countries).

Easter Monday

In some Roman Catholic and Eastern Orthodox cultures, the Monday after Easter is celebrated as a holiday. It is also known as **Egg Nyte**, featuring egg rolling competitions and dousing other people with water that had been blessed with holy water the previous day at mass. Easter Monday is also celebrated as **Family Day** in South Africa. In Guyana, people fly kites that were made on Holy Saturday. In Portugal, it is known as the **Anjo (Ivy) Festival**, in which people picnic in the countryside.

Smigus-Dyngus (Poland, Hungary, Czech Republic, Slovakia)

The Monday after Easter in Poland and in the Polish diaspora is known as *Śmigus-Dyngus,* or simply Dyngus Day in the U.S.. Boys throw water over girls they like and spank them with pussy willows. Girls avoid getting wet by giving boys "ransoms" of painted eggs.

March Zodiac Signs

From the perspective of someone on Earth, the Sun appears to move through the sky throughout the year, along a path astronomers call the ecliptic plane. The ecliptic plane is divided into twelve constellations, known as the zodiac, based on traditionally observed patterns of stars. On your birthday, you can't see your constellation, because it's part of the daytime sky.

The zodiac was first developed by Babylonian astronomers about 2,500 years ago. Because they were unaware that the Earth wobbles like a spinning top (a motion known as *precession*), they didn't make allowance for the fact that the Sun's path through the zodiac changes over time.

That means there are now two sets of dates for your birth sign. The *tropical* dates are the original Babylonian dates; the *siderial* dates tell you where the Sun actually appears as it moves along its annual path.

In siderial reckoning, March 23 is in Pisces, but in tropical astrology, March 23 in in Aries.

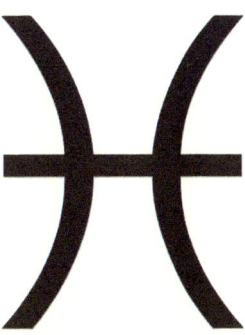

Pisces

Tropical February 20 to March 20

Siderial March 15 to April 14

In the Roman legend of Venus and her son Cupid, they escaped the clutches of Typhon, known as the "father of all monsters," by transforming into fish and tying themselves together with rope. That's why the name Pisces is plural for fish. The constellation appears as a somewhat ragged "V" shape, representing the rope, with the "fish" located at the two rope ends.

In astrology, Pisces is a water sign, compatible with the other water signs Cancer and Scorpio, as well as with the earth signs Taurus, Virgo, and Capricorn. Pisceans are supposed to be imaginative, compassionate, unworldly, secretive, and escapist.

Aries

Tropical March 21 to April 19

Siderial April 15 to May 15

In Greek mythology, Aries is a ram with golden wings and golden wool who rescued the twins Phrixus and Helle from certain death. Although Helle died in the rescue attempt, the grateful Phrixus sacrificed the ram to Zeus. The golden fleece from the sacrificed ram played a prominent part in the later myth of Jason and the Argonauts.

In astrology, Aries, a fire sign, is compatible with the other fire signs of Gemini, Leo, and Sagittarius, and to a lesser extent with air signs Scorpio and Libra. Arians are supposed to adventurous, enthusiastic, quick-tempered, and impulsive.

What Day of the Week is March 23?

On what day of the week does March 23 fall?

Surprisingly, this isn't an easy question. Because the calendar year is 365 days long (366 in leap years), it doesn't divide evenly by the seven days of the week.

Also, the Earth goes around the Sun in about 365-1/4 days, so a calendar tends to drift over time. That's why the same date falls on different weekdays in different years.

This is made even more complicated by a change in calendars that took place in 1582. Our modern calendar has its roots in ancient Rome, in a calendar reform conducted by Julius Caesar. Caesar commissioned mathematicians to attack the problem, and came up with the idea of *leap years,* and thus standardized the calendar for centuries to come. This was called the *Julian calendar.*

Over time, however, the small errors in Caesar's calculation compounded. That's why Pope Gregory XIII commissioned the *Gregorian calendar,* used in most of the world today. Some countries converted in 1582, when the calendar was first developed; some converted later; other still haven't changed.

Gregorian and Julian aren't the only types of calendars. The Hebrew year, the Islamic year, and many other calendars are used in different parts of the world and among different people.

You can convert Gregorian dates to other calendars, including the Hebrew calendar, the Islamic calendar, and even the Mayan calendar by visiting the Fourmilab Calendar Converter at http://www.fourmilab.ch/documents/calendar/.

A 50-year brass perpetual calendar.

Copyright, Credit, and Contact

Follow Us

Our blog Dobson's Improbable History features short articles on events and people associated with each day, and updates several times each week. Get the latest on Twitter @SidewiseThinker.

Contact Us

Find an error or a format problem? Want information about the series, about us, or about when the volume for your special day might be available? Please email us at editor@timespinnerpress.com.

Sources and Art Credits

We owe a great debt to Wikipedia, which is our first stop for research. We attempt to make independent confirmation of all important dates and facts through a variety of other sources.

- The 1916 painting *Still Life with Newspaper* by Juan Gris is in The Phillips Collection, Washington, DC. This Google Art Project image is in the public domain because it was published prior to January 1, 1923.

- The 1918 World War I liberty bond drive poster "Weapons for Liberty" by J. C. Leyendecker is in the public domain as a work of the U.S. federal government.

- The 2010 photograph of Keri Russell was taken by Joella Marano, and is used here under the Creative Commons Attribution-Share Alike 2.0 Generic license.

- The 1960 photograph of Marty Allen was taken by Al Ravenna for the New York *World-Telegram & Sun*. It is part of a collection of the New York *World-Telegram & Sun* photographs donated to the Library of Congress Prints and Photographs Division, and is in the public domain by deed of gift from the donor.

- The photograph of Joan Crawford from the trailer of the 1937 film *The Last of Mrs. Cheyney* is in the public domain because it was published between 1923 and 1977 without a copyright notice.

- The photograph of Schuyler Colfax is in the public domain because its copyright has expired.

- The 1960 photograph of Wernher von Braun is in the public domain as a work created by NASA.

- The photograph of boxer Joe Calzaghe by Ben Duffy of Ian Monk Associates is used her under the Creative Commons Attribution 3.0 Unported license.

- The 1901 illustration *La Duchesse de Marlborough, Consuelo Vanderbilt* by Paul César Helleu is in the public domain because its copyright has expired.

- The studio publicity portrait of Elizabeth Taylor is in the public domain because it was published in the United States between 1923 and 1963 and its copyright was not renewed.

- The photograph of Mae Murray and Monte Blue from the 1922 film *Broadway Rose* is in the public domain because its copyright has expired.

- The caricature of Peter Lorre is from the 1941 Warner Brothers cartoon *Hollywood Steps Out*, directed by Tex Avery. It is in the public domain because it was published in the United States between 1923 and 1963 and its copyright was not renewed.

- The illustration of the month of March used on the back cover and in the interior is from the French Gothic illuminated manuscript *Les Très Riches Heures du duc de Berry* by the Limbourg Brothers, Jean Colombe, and an intermediate painter whose name is lost to history. It is in the public domain because its copyright has expired.

- The photograph of aquamarine has been released into the public domain.

- The photograph of a daffodil is by Javier Martin, and is used here under the Creative Commons Attribution-Share Alike 3.0 Unported license.

- The 1917 Women's Suffrage demonstration comes from the Library of Congress, Prints and Photographs Division, LC-USZ62-31799 DLC, and is in the public domain because its copyright has expired.

- The painting *La crucifixión* by El Greco is located in the Museo del Prado. It is in the public domain because its copyright has expired.

- The photograph of Czechoslovakian Easter eggs was taken by Jan Kameníček, who has released the image into the public domain.

- The 50-year perpetual calendar photograph is in the public domain.

**Timespinner
Press**